Meow 680Q ?.00

D0517022

Arches National

by Day & Night

Text & photography by Grant Collier

Collier Publishing
Lakewood, CO

©2010, 2012 Grant Collier   ISBN # 978-097692188-2   Published by Collier Publishing LLC
Design by Grant Collier   Printed in China   http://www.collierpublishing.com

This book may not be reproduced in full or in part by any means (with the exception of short quotes for purpose of review) without permission of the publisher.

Many thanks to Dax Oliver and Catamount Mayhugh, who gave me feedback on the text.

Above Photo: South Window is seen from a viewpoint along Salt Wash.
Title Page: Venus and the Milky Way rise above Turret Arch on an autumn night.
Cover: View of Double Arch through Cove Arch in Cove of Caves.
Back Cover: Stars of the Milky Way provide a stunning backdrop to Balanced Rock.
Author photo taken by Jose' Low.

References:
http://www.nps.gov/arch/
Collier, Grant, *Colorado: Yesterday & Today*. Lakewood, CO: Collier Publishing LLC, 2001.
Doelling, Hellmut H, *Geology of Arches National Park*. Salt Lake City, UT: Utah Geological and Mineral Survey, 1985.
Johnson, David W, *Arches: The Story Behind the Scenery*. Las Vegas, NV: KC Publications, Inc., 1997.

About the Author

Grant Collier grew up in the foothills above Denver and spent much of his childhood exploring Colorado's Rocky Mountains. Grant first took up photography while attending college in Los Angeles. He found endless photographic opportunities in Moab and the Desert Southwest while driving to and from L.A. After graduating from college in 1996, Grant began a photographic career that had him following, quite literally, in the footsteps of his great-great-grandfather, the pioneer photographer Joseph Collier. Grant traveled throughout Colorado taking photos from the exact same spots that Joseph had taken his images over one-hundred years earlier. These photographs were published in the book *Colorado: Yesterday & Today*,

which was released in 2001. Since this time, Grant has continued exploring the Colorado wilderness, taking thousands of color nature photographs. These images have been published in many books, including *Colorado: Moments in Time, Colorado's Hidden Wonders, and Colorado's National Parks & Monuments*. Grant also produces a Colorado wall calendar, and his work appears in magazines across the United States and art galleries throughout Colorado. Grant has several other photography books in the works, including a coffee-table book on the Colorado Plateau and an instructional book on night photography. More information on Grant's photography can be found at: gcollier.com and collierpublishing.com.

Arches National Park

Eagle Park

Klondike Bluffs

• Tower Arch

• Marching Men

Salt Valley Wash

Devils Garden

• Double-O Arch

• Navajo Arch
• Landscape Arch
• Pine Tree Arch

• Skyline Arch

• Broken Arch

• Sand Dune Arch

Fiery Furnace

• Delicate Arch

• Wolfe Ranch

Cache Valley Wash

Salt Wash

• Eye of the Whale Arch

• Garden of Eden

Balanced Rock

• Double Arch

• North Window
• South Window

Turret Arch •

The Windows

Rock Pinnacles

The Great Wall

Petrified Dunes

Courthouse Wash

Tower of Babel •

Courthouse Towers

Three Gossips • • The Organ

Visitor Center

Colorado River

191

128

N

1 mile

Contents

Photographer's Notes

My passion for photography began in 1993 during my first trip to Arches National Park. I quickly fell in love with the alien landscape of arches, balanced rocks, fins, and spires. Although I scarcely knew what I was doing, I doggedly hiked to and photographed nearly every arch that appeared on the visitor's map. The spectacular scenery I discovered along the way and the good light and clouds I stumbled upon caused me to fall into the delusion that I was already a talented photographer.

After that first visit to Arches, I turned my attention to photographing in Colorado. Over the past eleven years, I have published seven photography books on the state. But now, my growing interest in night photography has reignited my passion for Arches National Park. There is, in my opinion, no better place on earth for night photography. Arches has some of the darkest night skies in North America and the sandstone rock formations offer a perfect complement to the starry skies.

In capturing photographs at night, I have not used any artificial light. I used the moon as my source of light to illuminate rock formations, and I shot on moonless nights to capture silhouettes of the sandstone monoliths against the night sky. I usually began the exposures one hour after sunset. At this time, there is still some ambient light and color in the sky that is not visible with the naked eye but that can be captured by the camera.

I used both film and digital cameras to capture the night shots. Most of the shots where the stars appear as curved lines, known as star trails, were taken with film. I set the aperture between f2.8 and f5.6 and exposed shots from five minutes to several hours. During the course of the exposure, the earth rotates on its axis, and the camera captures the movement of the stars across the sky.

All of the shots where the stars appear as points of light were taken with a digital camera. I set the ISO between 800 and 6400 and set the aperture between f1.4 and f2.8. By using high ISOs and a wide aperture, I was able to capture these low-light scenes with exposures under 40 seconds. The stars don't have much time to move across the sky during such a short exposure and thus appear as points of light.

I have done minimal alterations to the shots after they were taken. I adjusted the contrast and saturation to optimize the images for printing. I also used software to help reduce some of the noise that is inherent in low-light digital photography. I have not added or removed anything from the scene of any of the images, and I have attempted to keep the printed images true to what the camera captured.

I hope you enjoy this unique view of Arches National Park that I have attempted to portray.

Grant Collier
Lakewood, CO

Introduction

In his classic book *Desert Solitaire*, Edward Abbey warned visitors not to come to Arches National Park. He wrote:

> *Do not jump in your automobile next June and rush out to the Canyon country hoping to see some of that which I have attempted to evoke in these pages. In the first place you can't see anything from a car; you've got to get out of the goddamned contraption and walk, better yet crawl, on hands and knees, over the sandstone and through the thornbush and cactus. When traces of blood begin to mark your trail you'll see something, maybe. Probably not. In the second place most of what I write about in this book is already gone or going under fast. This is not a travel guide but an elegy. A memorial.*

Despite this warning, Abbey's passionate and evocative descriptions of the canyon country have drawn far more visitors than they have deterred. Today, during peak season, Arches National Park has turned into Abbey's worst nightmare. There are lines of cars that, at times, resemble rush hour traffic. The visitor center is packed with tourists from throughout the world, and masses of people, one behind the other, fill the path to Delicate Arch. But each night, after the sun goes down, Arches National Park returns to that primordial eden that Abbey so loved. Visitors gradually make their way back to Moab, leaving the roads and walkways all but empty. Silence returns to the park and the sandstone monoliths reassert their dominance over the landscape. Thousands of stars come out and provide a celestial display that can be found in few other places in the United States.

This is the Arches that I have come to love. It is an Arches that I have been fortunate to experience more than most people ever will. I have spent countless hours photographing the raw beauty of Arches' rock formations beneath a canopy of stars. When I am shooting film and exposing shots for hours at a time, I am able to sit back beneath an immense sandstone formation and contemplate heaven and earth.

On a clear night in Arches, I am able see nearly 3,000 stars, each of which is unfathomably large and inconceivably distant. I can view planets like Venus, Mars, and Jupiter as they gradually move across the night sky against the changeless backdrop of the constellations. Over the course of several nights, I can watch the moon gradually wax or wane, as it makes its faithful journey around Earth once every month. And if I am lucky enough to be at Arches during a meteor shower, I can watch as small interstellar debris repeatedly crashes into Earth's atmosphere, heats up, and ignites in brilliant fireballs that we call shooting stars.

Although the night sky is perhaps the most incredible sight that any of us will ever see, many of us take it for granted, as we are cut off from the natural world at night. We spend our nights watching television or working on a computer, ignoring a far more prodigious spectacle right above our rooftops. This was not the case for those who came before us. The Native Americans experienced the celestial display of the moon, stars, and planets on a nightly basis. To them, the heavens were even more unknown and unknowable than they are today, but they revered and studied them nonetheless. They often attributed moon phases and the position of the stars and planets to the gods and believed celestial events foretold their own earthly destiny.

There is, of course, an impassable chasm of time between us and these prehistoric inhabitants. But when I spend hours photographing alone in the desert, I can begin to understand the lives of the Native Americans. Their lives were inextricably tied to the desert landscape, and they depended on the vagaries of Mother Nature for their survival. They had to understand every nuance of the environment and utilize this knowledge to acquire the food, water, and shelter they depended on. While we can never have such a connection with the land today, we can at least reconnect with a primordial spirit that lives on in the Desert Southwest.

Although I believe summer nights are the ideal time to experience Arches in its most primal form, I have also grown to love the winters there. During the day, I am able find silence and solitude at all but the most popular formations. And the snowstorms in the desert are something to behold. They can blow in within minutes, ensconcing the park in deep fog and snow that renders all but the closest rock formations invisible. The storms can depart as quickly as they arrived, leaving behind pure white snow that adds immeasurable beauty to the red desert landscape.

Sometimes, after spending so much time alone in Arches, I begin to feel a certain possessiveness towards the park. I become overwhelmed by the crowds that inevitably reappear every spring. Unlike Edward Abbey, however, I will not warn people to stay away. The only Arches I have ever experienced is the one that exists today. I can not rail against losing that which I have never known. I have other places I can visit to find undisturbed beauty and absolute solitude. And despite Abbey's claims, all is not lost in Arches. There is still a magic that pervades the landscape. Just wait until after the sun goes down, turn off your flashlight, walk by moonlight across the sandstone, and spend hours gazing up at the stars through an immense natural arch. Then you'll see something. Maybe.

The faint glow of dusk illuminates a sandstone bowl below Delicate Arch.

A meteor streaks across the sky above Landscape Arch in Devils Garden

Left: The Organ in Courthouse Towers looms above a group of mule's ears in early May.

Right: Tower Arch frames spectacular desert scenery in Klondike Bluffs.

Left: The setting sun illuminates Tapestry Arch
on a cold winter day.

Right: The snow-covered La Sal Mountains
provide a spectacular backdrop to sandstone fins
in Fiery Furnace.

The moon rises between sandstone fins.

The moon, Venus, and Jupiter converge above Three Gossips.

Double Arch is seen through Cove Arch in Cove of Caves shortly after sunset.

16

Left: The Big Dipper is visible above rock formations in Park Avenue.

Right: Stars of the Milky Way rise above Marching Men in Klondike Bluffs.

An ultra-wide panoramic photo shows the entire band of he Milky Way above rock formations in Garden of Eden

Mesmeric patterns have formed in a rock formation in a remote part of the park.

Lightning bolts strike during an intense thunderstorm in late summer.

Left: A naturally-formed, fifty-foot-long tunnel through sandstone is found in a remote part of the park.

Right: Stars are visible through Serpentine Arch in Garden of Eden.

Above: Cottonwood trees stand alongside a canyon wall in Courthouse Wash.

Right: Dramatic fall colors are reflected in Courthouse Wash in late October.

Balanced Rock is reflected in a large puddle created after extremely heavy rains.

The late afternoon sun illuminates Eye of the Whale Arch.

Geology

Geology teaches us of the impermanence of all things. Over millions of years, seas advance and retreat, mountain ranges rise and fall, and land masses move across the globe. Most of these processes occur over such vast lengths of time that they are difficult to fathom. But in Arches National Park, geologic processes occur on a much shorter scale. In 1940, a large boulder fell out of Skyline Arch, doubling the size of the opening. During the winter of 1975-76, A Chip off the Old Block, which stood alongside Balanced Rock, fell over. In 1991 and again in 1995, large slabs of sandstone fell off of Landscape Arch. And in 2008, Wall Arch collapsed. Geology seems to be happening before our very eyes, transforming it from an abstract concept to a very real and immediate occurrence.

Although the natural arches began forming less than two million years ago, the rock and salt layers that form the foundation for the arches were first deposited approximately 300 million years ago. At this time, seas covered Paradox Basin, which occupies parts of southeastern Utah and southwestern Colorado. When the water ultimately retreated, it left behind layers of salt thousands of feet thick.

Over millions of years, numerous sediments were deposited on top of the salt layers. These sediments eventually compacted into sandstone. The oldest sandstone that is prominent in Arches is rounded, dome-shaped Navajo Sandstone, which is believed to have formed from sands of a large desert, similar to the Sahara, that once covered this region.

On top of the Navajo Sandstone is the Entrada Sandstone. This sandstone originated from deposits of tidal flats, beaches, and

Entrada Sandstone formations stand atop Navajo Sandstone.

sand dunes formed by an arm of a sea that once covered central Utah. Several different types of sandstone were later deposited above the Entrada Sandstone, but most of this rock has eroded away.

At one point, the sandstone overlying the salt layers may have been over one mile thick. The weight from this sandstone caused the salt layers to flow to areas of lower pressure. This movement forced some rock layers to be thrust upwards into geologic formations known as anticlines. One such anticline was the Salt Valley Anticline, which cuts across present-day Arches National Park.

The upper part of the salt beds beneath the Salt Valley Anticline eventually eroded away, causing the rock layers above to collapse. This collapse resulted in the creation of Salt Valley and Cache Valley. It also widened vertical cracks in the sandstone on the edge of the valleys. Erosion of these cracks formed what are known as fins in the Entrada Sandstone. These fins were eventually chiseled into the arches and spires that are seen today.

All of the major arches in the park have formed in Entrada Sandstone. The fins are eroded by rain, snow, and ground water, which dissolve the natural cement holding the sand grains together. In the winter, water seeps into cracks in the rock, then freezes and expands, thereby accelerating erosion. Oftentimes, rounded chunks of rock erode and fall off Entrada Sandstone. This can create overhangs in the rock, which eventually become arches.

Arches generally begin as small holes, or windows, in the rocks. When these openings expand to more than three feet in width or height, they are classified as arches. There are currently over 2,000 arches catalogued in Arches National Park,

Two of the most famous natural arches in the park are Landscape Arch and Delicate Arch. Landscape Arch is the largest arch in the park, and it is the longest arch in the world. It spans 290 feet and is only 6 feet thick at its narrowest point. Delicate Arch is the most recognized arch in the world and has become an icon of Utah and the American West. Unlike most other arches, it is entirely free-standing. The fin from which it has formed has almost completely eroded away, leaving only this extraordinary arch standing atop a sandstone bowl.

In addition to arches formed in fins, called vertical arches, there are also arches that form at cliff edges, called pothole arches or horizontal arches. These arches are formed in the same manner as vertical arches, but the rock is eroded downward near the edge of the cliff. An example of this type of arch is Double Arch, located in the Windows section. This rock formation likely began as a small pothole that eventually eroded down into two immense arches. There is also a smaller horizontal arch, called Pothole Arch, located northwest of Double Arch.

Other impressive natural wonders found in Arches National Park are balanced rocks. These are generally created where the Dewey Bridge Member of the Entrada Sandstone meets the Slickrock Member. Dewey Bridge Sandstone erodes more easily than Slickrock, and thus the formation becomes top-heavy as the lower part of the rock formation wears away. This can cause the formation to tilt slightly to one side. The Dewey Bridge Sandstone becomes more compact on the side where the tilting occurs. This causes the other side to erode more quickly, and thus the formation begins to tilt in the other direction. This process can repeat over and over, creating rocks that seem to be very precariously balanced.

A prime example of a balanced rock, and a centerpiece of Arches National Park, is the aptly-named Balanced Rock. The boulder that is perched atop the Dewey Bridge pedestal is approximately 50 feet high and weighs nearly 3,500 tons.

The fate of all the rock formations in Arches is the same. Erosive forces will slowly wear away at the Entrada Sandstone, causing the formations to eventually collapse. As this occurs, other unique and equally impressive formations will be created. The whole cycle will continue until all of the Entrada Sandstone has been eroded and washed into the Colorado River, thus ending an extraordinary period of geologic activity at Arches National Park.

Tower of Babel is seen through Baby Arch in Courthouse Towers.

The last light of day illuminates Sheep Rock in Courthouse Towers.

Left: Star trails from a two-hour exposure cross above a rock formation in Klondike Bluffs.

Right: An unusual rock formation in Klondike Bluffs is lit by the full moon on a spring night.

Left: The setting sun illuminates rock formations in seldom-visited Eagle Park.

Right: Patterns of mud and moss formed along the bottom of Courthouse Wash during a dry spell.

An ultra-wide panoramic photo shows both openings of Double Arch in the Windows section.

Tower Arch is seen from an alcove in the Klondike Bluffs section.

Clouds float above sandstone fins near Sand Dune Arch on an autumn night.

Above: Broken Arch stands beneath a canopy of stars on a summer night.

Left: The branches of a dead pinyon pine are silhouetted against the night sky.

A thin cloud floats beneath the La Sal Mountains, which rise high above the national park.

A large cumulus cloud hovers above sandstone fins during the late summer monsoon season.

Picturesque clouds float above Skyline Arch on a winter afternoon.

Left: Sandstone formations in Courthouse Towers are seen through a seldom-visited arch located high atop a cliff face.

Right: Large boulders are scattered in front of Covert Arch, which is located in a new and secluded part of the park.

Above: The late-afternoon sun illuminates Double O Arch in Devils Garden.
Left: Countless stars are seen above the rock formations of Park Avenue.

Left: Mule's ears grow in the park in early May.

Right: Common paintbrush thrive near Courthouse Wash in early May.

Flora & Fauna

At first glance, Arches National Park may seem like a barren and lifeless place filled with immense sandstone formations and little else. But in truth, life thrives in the park. This life has adapted to a harsh environment that experiences relentless summer heat and blinding winter snowstorms.

There are over 50 species of mammal in Arches National Park. Most of them are nocturnal, and thus few visitors ever see all of the life that abounds in this landscape. Among the nocturnal mammals are kangaroo rats, skunks, foxes, and bobcats.

The cottontail is found throughout Arches National Park.

The largest mammals in the park are mule deer, desert bighorn, and mountain lions. The mule deer are the most commonly seen of these animals, while sightings of mountain lions are very rare.

When the Native Americans lived here, approximately two million desert bighorn inhabited the Southwest. However, bighorn are extremely vulnerable to livestock disease, and their population dropped precipitously after white settlers arrived in the late 1800s. By 1975, there were only about 1,000 desert bighorn left in Utah and none resided in Arches National Park.

Bighorn have made a comeback in recent years. In the early 1980s, desert bighorn were relocated from Canyonlands National Park to Arches National Park. Today, there are an estimated 75 bighorn in Arches and approximately 3,000 in Utah.

Reptiles are also frequently seen in the park. The most common is the lizard, and species found in Arches include the northern whiptail, the desert spiny, and the western collared lizard. There are also several different snake species in Arches, most of which are non-venomous. The exception is the midget-faded rattlesnake, which has very toxic venom but will attempt to avoid human contact.

Arches has a surprisingly large and varied population of frogs, toads, and salamanders. These tenacious amphibians lay their eggs in any water source they can find, including potholes, springs, and intermittent streams like Courthouse Wash and Salt Wash.

Birds are the most commonly seen animal in Arches National Park. 273 different bird species have been recorded in the park. Among these birds is the raven, a remarkably intelligent bird that is found throughout the Desert Southwest. Another bird that has been spotted in Arches is the American peregrine falcon. The use of DDT as a pesticide pushed the peregrine to the brink of extinction in the 1970s. It has made a comeback in recent years and was removed from the endangered species list in 1999.

Like most deserts, Arches is also prime habitat for insects and arachnids. These include mosquitoes, scorpions, black widow spiders, and tarantulas.

All of the animal life in Arches is dependent, in one way or another, on the plant life that grows there. The largest plant in the park is the Fremont cottonwood, which generally grows along washes, such as Courthouse Wash. The most common trees are pinyon pines and junipers. These trees are ideally suited for Arches National Park, since they are able to grow in dry, rocky terrain.

Another plant that is well adapted to the climate is the cactus. Nine species of cacti grow in Arches, including the prickly pear and claret cup, which sprout brilliant flowers in the spring.

Numerous other wildflowers blossom each year in April and May. Wildflower populations vary significantly from year to year, as the flowers are heavily dependent on seasonal rainfall. Among the most common flowers are paintbrush, mule's ears, and mountain pepperplant.

Grasses found in the park include ricegrass, needle-and-thread, galleta, blue grama, and cheat grass. Cheat grass is a non-native species that has infiltrated much of the American West.

Since Arches has so much exposed sandstone, lichens and mosses are able to thrive. These primitive plants also make up part of the biological soil crust, which can be found throughout Arches National Park. This crust, which consists mostly of cyanobacteria, is perhaps the most vital part of the park's ecosystem.

Cyanobacteria bind particles in the soil together, making the ground surface resistant to erosion. This, in turn, allows larger plant life to take root and grow in the hardened crust. Cyanobacteria are also able to convert atmospheric nitrogen into a form that plants can use, and the soil crust stores water and nutrients for the plants.

The web of life that has formed in Arches National Park is simultaneously fragile and robust. Individual species have been driven to the brink of extinction by human activity. The destruction of the biological crust has lead to the reduction of plant life and, in turn, put stress on wildlife populations. But, as it does everywhere on Earth, life in Arches will always find a way to adapt and thrive. And even as some human endeavors have threatened life in the park, other initiatives have helped repair this damage. One look at an agile desert bighorn on a rocky cliff face or a lone peregrine falcon soaring over the desert attests to the fact that people can live in harmony with this remarkable landscape.

Left: A mule deer stands in a valley below Landscape Arch in Devils Garden.

Right: Pinyon pine and juniper trees are seen through the northern opening of Anniversary Arch in Klondike Bluffs.

Left: Mountain pepperplant grows in profusion along Salt Valley Road.

Right: A yucca plant grows along a sandy hillside in Klondike Bluffs.

Left: Surprise Arch is hidden inside a maze of rock fins known as Fiery Furnace.

Right: Ring Arch is a rarely-visited rock formation located near Courthouse Wash.

Above: The full moon illuminates Ribbon Arch in the Windows section.

Right: The planet Venus makes up part of a celestial display above a balanced rock in Garden of Eden.

The last light of day illuminates Delicate Arch.

Above: Flowers blossom from a cactus in mid-May.
Right: View of Sand Dune Arch in Fiery Furnace.

Star trails are seen through the openings of Double Arch in the Windows section

Numerous stars trails are visible through Pine Tree Arch, as the stars rotate arour ?

The vibrant glow of dusk illuminates remote rock formations beneath the snow-covered La Sal Mountains.

Left: Dramatic rays of light shine over Balanced Rock as the sun emerges from behind a cloud.

Right: A narrow light beam penetrates into a dark rock cave in Fiery Furnace.

Dramatic rock formations in Garden of Eden are silhouetted against star trails on an autumn night.

Star trails rise above Skyline Arch and a pinyon pine.

Leaping Arch lies beneath numerous star trails.

Above: A yucca plant grows near the southern opening of Anniversary Arch in Klondike Bluffs.

Right: View of Courthouse Wash Rock Art, located in the far southern part of the park.

Human History

The natural arches, fins, spires, and balanced rocks in Arches National Park combine to form a landscape unlike any other in the world. Today, nearly one million people come to this park each year to witness these incredible rock formations.

Given the scant archaeological evidence, it is difficult to know how long humans have marveled at these natural wonders. But it is possible that many thousands of years ago, humans laid eyes on an immense, but thicker and less eroded Landscape Arch. They might have seen Delicate Arch when a bit more of the sandstone fin from which it eroded was intact. And they may have witnessed an immense natural arch that geologists believe once connected Sheep Rock to a large sandstone fin to its southwest.

The first people known to live in the vicinity of Arches National Park were the Paleo-Indians, who arrived 10,000 years ago. They used the area to make stone tools, such as dart points, knives, and scrapers. They are thought to have been big-game hunters and their culture existed until around 6000 B.C.

Succeeding the Paleo-Indians in Utah were the Archaic people. These inhabitants relied more on small game and wild plants for food. Archaeologists have found a few spear points, campsites, and rock art from the Archaic people within Arches National Park.

Approximately 2,000 years ago, the Anasazi and Fremont Indians infiltrated much of the Desert Southwest. These Native Americans introduced farming to the region. Around

Ute Indians carved petroglyphs near Wolfe Ranch.

1100 AD, the Anasazi Indians moved their villages from mesa tops to protective rock overhangs along canyon walls. They inhabited these dwellings for less than two centuries, after which they and the Fremont Indians mysteriously vanished from the region.

Both the Anasazi and Fremont Indians are thought to have often passed through Arches, as the park lies on the boundary between the two cultures. Like the Paleo-Indians and Archaic people, these tribes used the area to craft stone tools. Some impressive rock art by these tribes, including the immense Courthouse Wash Panel, can be found in Arches. Arches also has at least one small granary built by the Anasazi, and there are some larger ruins in nearby Canyonlands National Park.

The vacancy left by the Anasazi and Fremont Indians around 1300 AD was filled by the Utes and Paiutes. These tribes subsisted primarily as hunters and gatherers. In the 1600s, the Utes acquired horses from the Spanish and became one of the most powerful tribes in the western United States.

The first European explorers to enter Utah were the Spanish, who came in search of travel routes from New Mexico to their California missions. They built the Old Spanish Trail, which extended from Santa Fe to Los Angeles and ran alongside Arches National Park. The Spanish used this trail from 1829-1848.

In the 1820s, trappers and traders also began exploring much of the western United States. The first known trapper to enter Arches National Park was Denis Julien who left the following inscription on a rock face: "Denis Julien, June 9, 1844."

In 1848, the Mexican War broke out between the United States and Mexico. Mexico offered little resistance to the American troops, and by 1849 they had surrendered the entire southwestern region of the present-day United States.

The first American settlement near Arches was built by Mormon pioneers, who established the Elk Mountain Mission in present-day Moab in June of 1855. However, conflict between the settlers and the Ute Indians caused the Mormons to quickly abandon their settlement.

In the 1880s, ranchers, prospectors, and farmers came to the area and created a permanent settlement in Moab. Amongst these settlers were a man named John Wesley Wolfe and his son Fred. John suffered from a leg injury inflicted during the Civil War and hoped that a drier climate would improve his condition. The two men built a small cabin near the current parking lot for the Delicate Arch trailhead. In 1906, they were joined by John's daughter, her husband, and their children. They built a new, larger cabin on the site that still exists today.

One of the earliest promoters of the red-rock country around Arches was Loren "Bish" Taylor, who took over the Grand Valley Times in Moab in 1911. Taylor often wrote about the incredible natural wonders he found while exploring the landscape around Moab.

In 1923, a prospector named Alexander Ringhoffer became enchanted by the sandstone monoliths north of Moab. He wrote the Rio Grande Western Railroad in an attempt to gain support for creating a national park. The railroad executives eagerly took up the idea, as they wanted to attract more passengers to the area. The government sent research teams to study the landscape, and on April 12, 1929 President Herbert Hoover established Arches National Monument. On November 12, 1971, Richard Nixon signed a bill from Congress designating Arches as a national park.

Since the creation of the national park, visitation to Arches has continually increased. The volume of visitors has forced park officials to find a balance between providing access to the rock formations and preserving the delicate landscape. Fortunately, while many of the largest arches see countless visitors each year, there is still spectacular scenery tucked away in remote areas of the park. This landscape remains much the same as it was when Native Americans first set foot in Arches thousands of years ago.

A mesa is reflected in the window of the Wolfe Ranch cabin, located near the Delicate Arch parking lot.

View of the entrance to the root cellar, which was used for storage at Wolfe Ranch.

Left: Clouds float above a pyramidal rock formation on a summer night.

Right: Magic Mystery Bridge is seen from a deep alcove behind the arch.

A large balanced rock sits perched atop its pedestal in a remote part of Arches called Eagle Park.

Logs are scattered along the opening of Navajo Arch in Devils Garden.

Above: Turret Arch is seen through North Window during a January snowstorm.

Left: Snow-covered rock formations in the Windows section are obscured by fog.

Left: Pine Tree Arch frames a pinyon Devils Garden.

Right: Picturesque clouds float above Arch in Devils Garden.

Above: Landscape Arch is illuminated by the rising sun shortly after the summer solstice.

Overleaf (left): A bizarre rock formation is silhouetted against the night sky in Devils Garden.
Overleaf (right): Star trails are seen through Tunnel Arch in Devils Garden.

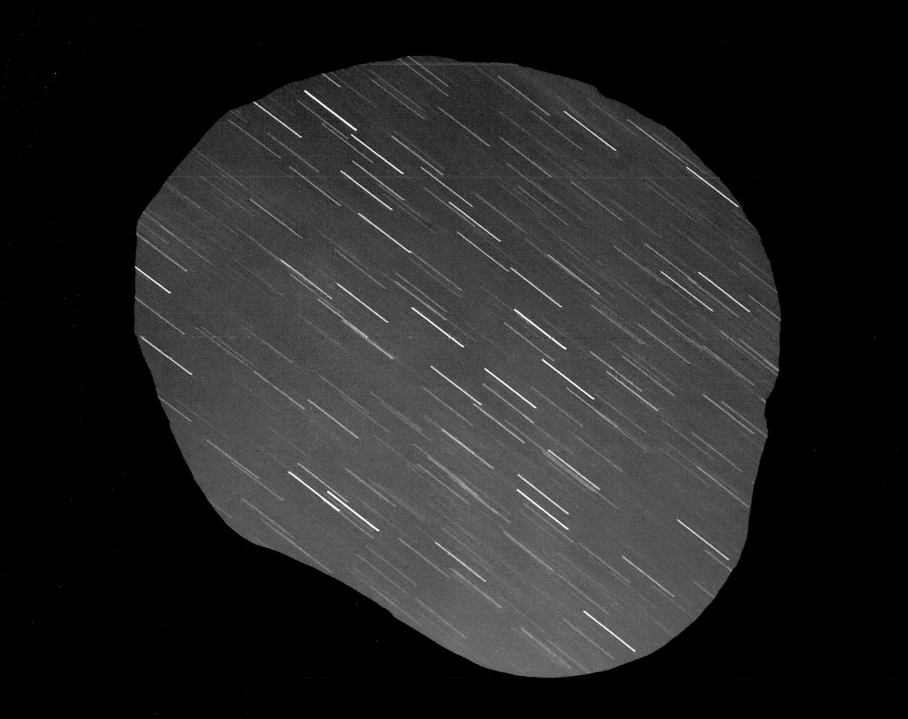

The Organ is reflected in a pothole in the Courthouse Towers section.

Three Gossips is reflected in a water-filled pothole that formed during heavy rains.

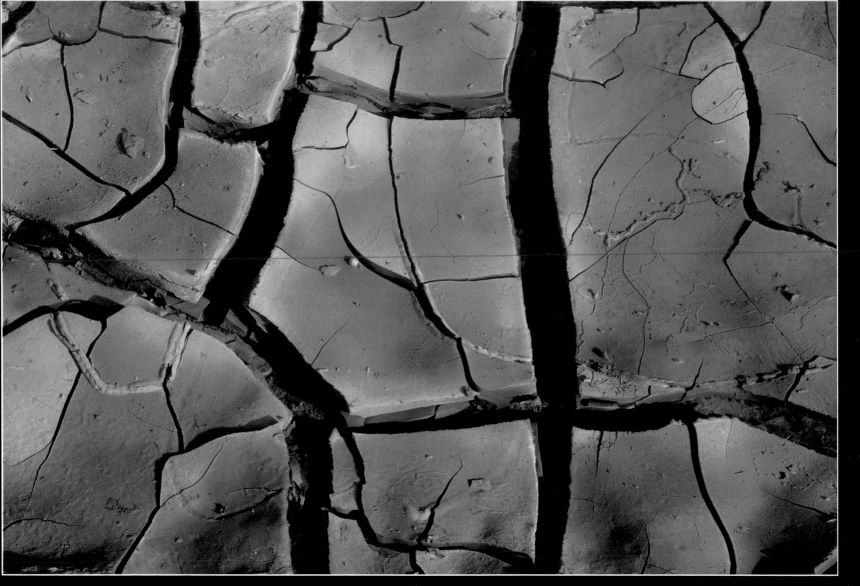

Intricate patterns have formed in cracked mud along Courthouse Wash.

A pothole reflects a sandstone fin in Fiery Furnace.

View from a narrow passage in Fiery Furnace.

Stars of the Milky Way provide a dramatic backdrop to the free-standing Delicate Arch.

The Milky Way rises above Balanced Rock, as the moon begins to rise on the left.

An ephemeral double rainbow rises above the Salt Creek area of Arches National Park.